On This Journey

On this Journey

Dr. Tameka "Doc" Wright

ISBN: 0692426981
ISBN-13: 978-0692426982

Published by: Humble Publishing

P.O. Box 9749

Newark DE. 19714

Introduction

Allow me to introduce to you this book of poetry that has been birthed out of my being. I hope that it will inspire, motivate and encourage you to proceed in life. Seat back while I take you "On this Journey"

Credentials

Diploma in Evangelism, Bachelor's in Divinity, Master's in Ministry, Doctorate in Pastoral Counseling and a Doctorate in Ministry.

For more information:

www.docwmusic.com

Email:

tahjent@gmail.com

Dedication

This book is dedicated to my Mom (Bonita Wright) and my Dad (Pastor Louis Saddler). Two special people who God entrusted to raise me into being the women I am today. They were very instrumental in my life and I loved them dearly.

R. I. P., Mommy and Daddy. I miss you. Love your little girl.

Table of Contents

Acknowledgements

I would like to recognize who made this all possible and that is My Lord, Jesus Christ. Without Him this would not be possible. Thank you Lord, for using me, as your vessel to deliver the Good News. I am forever grateful and humbled that you would use Me in this way. I draw on this scripture: If you abide in Me, and my words abide in you, you will ask what you desire, and It shall be done for you (John 15:7).

On This Journey

I was created out of misery and strife

I have been saved by my Lord Jesus Christ

Existed through suffering and pain

Remained because my Father reigns

Was isolated and beat because of my beliefs

But my Savior came and gave me peace

Don't expect handouts, worked hard for what I get

Followed the light that He so delicately has lit

The pathway is long and concerning

Learn of me

As I feed your eyes "On This Journey"

My Life

I cry the tears

My momma was too afraid to cry

I bore the shame

That was too evident to claim

Family portrait in a frame

Standing by while living a lie

Eating soup in a can to get by

The funny thing is I never asked why

Maybe because I was too shy

Or too

Shameful

Embarrassed

By the shear fact of my

Existence

To complicate matters more

My skin was a shade different than expected

One that was not accepted

Left with emptiness, no way to express

Bottled up ready to ignite

Light it up

Watch it take flight

The Breath of Life

Listen

Can you hear

The silence

Of the

Atmosphere

No sound is made

Peaceful as the day long

The only sound playing

Is my heartbeat song

Blood making it pump

Hear the thump, thump

Listening closer

The breath of life

In-hale, exhale

Time

Stalling for time

Letting the clock unwind

It tells of a story

Before the beginning of time

I can remind

You

Of that time

When the seconds turned into minutes

The higher the hand climbed

Although it twisted and turned

To strike the middle

It takes more to unravel this riddle

So when you're looking at time

Keep in your mind

That your seconds, turn into minutes

In a matter of time

It's All Mental

What are Pain, Depression and Confusion....

Other than a mental distraction

Keeping you from your God given destiny

Don't give the enemy the satisfaction

Stay focused on the true and Living God

Because in His wings, it's you He will hide

Being misled, manipulated and misinformed

Is how the enemy preys

Having an appearance like a tropical storm

Behind the winds is where he lays

Playing tricks with your mind

What a clever charade

Waiting to attack you from your blind side

Give up Satan there is nowhere to hide

The fight is on, gear up to do battle

Put on your helmet of salvation

Your breastplate of righteous

Grab your shield of faith

Along with your sword of the Spirit

Your full armor of God is what is needed

Cause the enemy doesn't even know that he is already defeated

Keep your eyes looking up

To the Kingdom of Heaven

Your mind stayed on Jesus

In that, peace will overcome you

And your Pain, Depression and Confusion

Will not last

It will only become a thing of the past

Ask Why

Why do we as Christians pretend we are ok?

When we are not

Why do we say let it rain?

When we really want it to stop

Why does God say He will take the pain away?

Yet we still hurt

Why do we pour our souls out?

When we should have stayed introverts

Could this be all a dream?

Things are really not what they seem

Fantasy now becomes truth

Evilness is now who we salute

No answers coming our way

No solutions, so now we have to pay

The price is high

Which money cannot buy

And it still leaves me with

This

Question

Why

Am I the Only One

Contemplating my next move

Thinking what I need to prove

To myself, to others, or people that don't understand

Trying to come up with the master plan

Do I go to the left or right?

Up or down

Let's say I play the middle to be safe

I can't do that because my feelings will be erased

Could this be a phase?

A misconception of the mind

I'm sinking fast and running out of time

I need to make my presence felt

My emotions known

Resolve my pain

This is a mystery

It's getting to me

Slow down take it easy I tell myself

"Am I the only one?"

Do I measure my self-worth

By what I'm feeling inside

By what people think

I'm still a strong, black, intelligent woman

So I must take control of my life

Demolish and Eliminate the Stress and Strife

What do I do I'm so confused

Things that were real are not reality anymore

God must have something better in store

So now I guess I will wait until my change comes

Until then, "Am I the only one?"

Recovering

I thank God for my words cause that's is how I get my point across

How I ease my pain, from being on the cross

I don't equivalent my suffering to my savior

Or excuse what comes up from my behavior

Just letting it be known, that this hurts so bad

Then the hurt turns into something that makes me mad

Not knowing is not always good

As not showing, then wishing you should

What comes up, I pray it heals

My heart is in a glass filled

The news of this in a broken glass that spills

As in my heartbeat that stands still

The table is covered with all my emotions

Overflowing into a gigantic ocean

Recovering

Beyond Limits

I'm stretched beyond limits

Pulled on every side

Chills running through my body

Making me feel paralyzed

The grammatical, expression

Keeps ya guessing

Pumping red blood cells

To ignite confession

Less then, no equal to

The equation, has you gazing

Makes you say she's simply amazing

I get deep, with the brain

So don't sleep

I sneak up on ya

Like I'm creep, creep

Wake up, no time for slippin

The intellect of the brain

Can't be tamed, I'm a rip it

Let the smoke clear

The signal to the coming

Watch it disappear

See the enemy running

I throw hits with my words

Biblical grammar

Unscramble

Paying homage to the Original Founder

Free

I take delight

In the fight, for freedom

I make moves

That are approved, if you see them

Be educated by the system

If you choose it

I take my cues from the book

So I won't lose it

Striving hard to make it right

Pay attention or pay the price

One day the shackles lifted

From the body

Then the mind

Souls are gifted

How can it explain

The pain

That was shifted

On to the next

Nothing left

But the reminiscence

Of self-respect

Take heed

To the greed

Of the world

Don't get caught

Up

Or down

Like the pants to

The ground

There is more

To explore

When released

From the mentality

Of the beast

Freedom comes

Freedom goes

Can we be free

From this system

That plagues

Our reality

Focus

Learn to focus

Get inspired

Make minds wonder

Stay tuned

Not confused

Don't go under

Searching for real life

Pay the price

Thoughts all scattered

It don't matter

Win or lose

Play the fool

You're still cool

Learn to focus

Many have come

Many have left

Some as family

Some as guest

Hurt stopped by

Pain did too

No clue

It would happen to you

In all

We must not forget

The way things happen

Is for the best

If you lose focus

You will find yourself in a mess

A Dream is a Dream

Should we go on making believe that

We have a dream

That in fact our dreams can come true

Look at the many people that have died

And their dreams did not come true

Should we go on setting goals

So far out of reach, that Gods arms cannot get close to

Just a figment of our imagination that we hold on to

Who is the real villain in all of this?

The one that gives us hope and bliss

Dreams are made but yet broken

By the reality that this is, the life

The life that was created before

Before we were even born

I for one have to start putting things in perspective

Why dream, only to be let down

Why have goals only to find out they will never be reached

There are some cases that are unique,

But the average person will not reach

Take a deep, look at your history

That is where there's a mystery

Just like my ancestors were sold

I too was sold, on the idea that I am free

How can I be free, with this modern day slavery

I will die with this dream inside

The world will not allow my dreams to come true

This is a lesson that needs to be learned too

I guess you cannot be mad, because this was already in place

My birth certificate said I was of the other race

Now to discover my life has no meaning

Well not for me anyway

We live to do work for the One that sent us

This earth I cannot stay

In time you will find out what I mean

Until then a Dream is a Dream

Rhythmic

I make erythematic decisions, according to the rhymes

I was born, way before my time

I hit switches, competition be missing

More cunning then the average politician

He Breathed in me, set the captives free

Broke the chains, had the master key

Does the cat got your tongue

I'm a make the naysayers numb

I serve the Ultimate One

Yea... and I have just begun

Before My Time

I keep feeding my soul with words to sink into my being

Hoping it will destroy the feeling inside

Not trying to hide, but to seek refuge

Under a pavilion is how it was explained

The fact still remains that I am striving, but still getting side tracked

From the things I was told or sold under the idea that it would come true

Still holding on to the dreams that once were visions

Visions, lead only in my head,

Trying to find an outlet to express the complexity of being mislead

Did I misled myself or was this something I was born

Was it told or was it an idea that was formed

The question still comes to mind

Am I before my time

Am I before my time

One would say yes, been here before

Came back cause there were somethings I had to address

Had to take on this body, So that it would manifest

Spirit was here but now I am here in the flesh

There is a plan we must carry out

The master plan, the plan from our Master

Blue print created for us to follow

Even sent to earth a magnificent model

So when I say am I... before my time

Doesn't mean physically but spiritually

I have been here before

Sent back now to win souls for Christ

Giving people the opportunity to get this thing right

Cause I know a man, a man named Jesus

He is the reason

The reason why I move, breath, live

It's all because of Him

Yes sir, yes ma'am I am before my time

Medication

How can medicine prescribed to help you,

End up hurting you

The more you pump in your body

The worse you get

I know some may think this is so far fetched

But think about it

How can medicine make you better?

It's just something to help you maintain

It may help one thing but then there are side affects

It will

Make another condition worse

Then you have to take more medicine to fix that

A never ending cycle, still no help

The pharmaceutical companies are getting richer

Well my body is getting weaker

Keep pumping this prescribed medicine

That is making me high

Keep pumping this prescribed medicine

That makes me deny

Keep pumping this prescribed medicine

The devil in a pill, a pump, aaaa pen

Pump it in

They Crucified Him

I wonder why you love me so

Beaten down

Risen from the grave

Just to let me know

Supernaturally is how you endured

You never said you couldn't take it no more

Like a hero you stood tall

Up on the hill they call the skull

The pain was deep

Right down to the core

Even when they beat you more and more

Pierced you in your side

Crowned your head with thorns

Blood came rushing down

What was going through your mind

Cause sin was not even found

A human couldn't take it

Mentally we can't even shake it

Can you fathom what our Savior has done

No human could have withstood this, No not one

Organize Yourself

What will it take

For you to make

A decision

On life

How you want to live it

Is it

Above the rim

Mid court

In between

Places not seen

Would you just be another

Player on the team

You dream

Of happiness and peace

At the same time

Inside you're fighting a beast

Deep some may say

That's the reality of life

Living in the hope

Of finding yourself

You can run

But you can't hide

Turn the corner

You're still facing you

Trying to come up with

What is true

Truth be told

An old lady is knocking at your door

Time is running out

Put your life in order

Focus on the task at hand

Reclaim your life

Take a stand

Empty

Tears flowing

For no reason

Could it be

There's too much people pleasing

No time for self

Just enough

Time

To make sure people are fine

No one should live like this

Where emotions

Don't even exist

Their feelings

You might as well forget

No time for those to be dealt with

Pain

From the misery imposed

Suffering

From the negativity I suppose

There is no Peace

Without justice

No happiness

Without hope

The outside represents

Strength, courage, power, prestige

The inside represents

A defeated mentality, shyness, a little girl crying

Asking why

Healing is in the process

Complete this person

A must

In God I

Must trust

Hear a Word

I want to hear You

Your every Word

Teach me

To distinguish the difference

They say prayer and fasting

Is a sure way to discover

Your voice

I will try it

To see what I come up with

In the meantime

I'm lost

Confused

The world is saying one thing

My inner being is saying another

Still I have not heard from You

Troubled

Perplexed

Can't sleep at night

Waiting up just to get a glimpse

Of You

In your Word

Is where they tell me the answers are

Lead me

Guide me

Feed me

Fill up this empty vessel

I need power to overcome

Shelter me

Protect me

Hide me

In Your pavilion

Strength is what I need

Endurance is what I strive for

I need to hear

A

Word

From you Lord

 A Word

Green Grass

The grass

Sometimes not greener on the other side

So you instead

Play

Both sides of the fence

Hoping one day one

Will be eliminated

The thrill

The adventure

The excitement

The adrenaline

Working

Flowing

The anticipation

Expectation

Quickly mounting

Higher

To a point of an explosion

What is left

Pick up the pieces

Of a once, happy life or was it

Light

To walk away

Is easier said than done

To leave behind

All your

Dreams

Goals

Aspirations

Things once hoped for

The light that once shined

Now being dim

Looks different

Do you

Go on with a dim light

Do you

Find a way for it to ignite

Or

Do you, Let it Burn Out

Tail Chaser

Running from yourself

To where

No one knows

Round and round

In circles

Tail chaser

Hiding behind

The former shell of yourself

Making excuses

For your actions

Bow

Your

Head

In shame

The person you once were

You're not anymore

What have you become

A tail chaser

Instead of being scared

Of society

And the evils of this world

Be scared of catching

Your

Tail

Ha Que 1

Focus on what you can do

And not what you can't do

Ha Que 2

Be smart with the

Gift

You were given

Work it until

You can't work it

No more

Use it or it will be

Lost

Ha Que 3

It doesn't matter

What you think of me

Your opinion doesn't count

I'm going to do

The will of God

Regardless

Ms. Karma

Life has a funny way of playing tricks

On you

What goes around

Comes around

Karma

What's good

Is not always

What's good for you

Now that you have seen

Ms. Karma

No face

No appearance of the norm

Just memories

Of what once was

Sweet, cunning

Coming when you least expect

You got what you

Deserved

Ms.

Karma

Full of Lies

Lies being told

Money made

Lies being told

Nothing gained

Lies being told

To suit needs

Lies being told

Where will this lead

Lies being told

You have convinced yourself

Lies being told

Until there is nothing left

ReBirth

God you are the Potter

I am the clay

Make me over again

Reform me

Reshape me

Back into the image

You created me

From the dust of the ground

You shaped me

Blew the breath

Of life

Into my body

You

Made me

A being

Three parts

Body

Soul

Spirit

My Father

I look the way I look

Because of who my father is

I suffer the way I suffer

Because of who my father is

I live the way I live

Because of who my father is

I endure the way I endure

Because of who my father is

I cry the way I cry

Because of who my father is

Look

Suffer

Live

Endure

Cry

All because

Of who my

Father

Is

Protected

If you can't help me

Please don't block me

Move to the side

Let me experience

The newness of life

The type

That's

Stress free

Drama free

Free to be me

See you can hurt this

Surface

Called the flesh

My spirit you can't touch

It's protected

By the essence

Of God

Shielding the insides

Take your best shot

Still not good enough

I get up

I'm not a weak individual

Nor do I give in

Come if you want to

I'm a sure win

You Said

You said, God:

You would give me peace that passes all understanding

You said, God:

I would have unspeakable joy

You said, God:

You would wipe the tears from my eyes

You said, God:

You would not put more on me then I could bear

You said, God:

Your love for me was for eternity

You said, God:

You would bring me through my struggles

You said, God:

You will be with me always

I will speak your words into existence

It's Final

They said I would not make it

They said I would not amount to anything

They talked about me

Lied on me

Mistreated me

I remember hearing

You're weak, you're soft

You're too kind

So I started falling

Into the mind set

Of believing what I heard

Passing up the opportunities

God had for me

Shutting the doors

God had opened for me

No more

I'm too strong, too bold

Walking through those doors

Not listening to the nay sayers

Look at me now

I have made it!

Emotions

Anger

Rage

Tension

Built up

Sadness

Sorrow

Despair

Filled up

Release to find

Joy

Peace

Happiness

You will feel the difference

Rose Petals

Does anybody pay attention

to a

Rose

that is dead

Withered

Brown

Drawn up

leaves fallen

on the outside of the vase

we call this world

It is so pretty

In full blossom

attractive to the eye

women long to receive it

all year round

especially on occasions

but this particular

Rose

can't be saved

try to gather

all the petals

into a circle

piece them back

together this Rose

needs to

Bloom again

Heart Felt

I write from the heart

Letting it all hang out

Using my pen as the weapon

Thoughts as power

My mind as the tool

Speak with boldness

Projecting the voice

Hear me

Feel me

as I come across

this is not your ordinary

Everyday

Traditional

Poetess

I won't say the typical things

expression is the key

to get to the point

Vibe with me

Simple

Is life as simple

as it is portrayed

Curves

Corners

somehow exist

the meaning

is as

Simple

as the word

not understood

easily mistaken

by the mere fact

that it can't

be explained

It's just the

way it

is

Simple

Still No Relief

Is the inevitable always reality

Does the good outweigh the bad

Do you learn from your experiences

Do you let excuses take over

pouring out your soul

you want to be listened to

cannot find a friend

so what do you do

still no relief

there is sorrow

a heavy load to carry

Why do the tears keep coming

that cannot be stopped

Why does there have to be pain

It's hitting home now

affecting the way life is lived

What is true love?

Is it even real

Does it exist

still no relief

Take a deep breath

let it exhale

change the thinking of the brain

from negative into a positive

Relief must be found

Church Time

It's Sunday morning

time for church

this is the place where you go

to get rid of all your pain

from lies to misbehaving

God is sure to forgive

He will free you from your sins

A healthy wholesome life is what we need

through Jesus Christ

our Antidote

there is praying and singing

preaching and teaching

all in one place

Souls being saved

Confused minds freed

Healing and Deliverance

Hallelujah Is the Highest Praise

For all that God has done

Shout hallelujah

He made a way out of no way

Shout hallelujah

For His protection

Shout hallelujah

For His deliverance

Shout hallelujah

For His healing

Shout hallelujah

For being a provider

Shout hallelujah

Pressure

If I ran away from home

Where would I go

to the streets

to a friend's house

to relatives

anywhere to escape

or hide

from the pressure of life

See dealing with pressure

is not my forte

not my stel lio

as they call it on the streets

pushing things to the side

Is what I did

now they're back to haunt me

disrupting

my fairy tale life

I just can't go out like that

giving into the pressure

I'm talking about

there has to be a solution

There is

I found refuge in writing

just to cope and get by

I figured

put it down on paper

so I can read it back

make sense of this whole thing

clear thoughts started coming

to my head

I found a new passion

Poetry

that is how I defeated

the

Pressure

You are the Reason

You are the reason:

I am who I am

You are the reason:

I have the strength to move

You are the reason:

I am not dead in sin

You are the reason:

I can make it

You are the reason:

I wake up every morning

You are the reason:

I can go on after being knocked down

You are the reason:

I am in the land of the living

You are the reason:

I can laugh when I feel like crying

You, Lord, are the reason

I give You all the praises due to You

Recipes

Believe in the unbelievable

Reach the unreachable

Love the unlovable

Soar higher than a butterfly

Trust the untrustable

Sing to the top of your lungs

Pray without ceasing

Have hope when there is nothing else

Show kindness to your enemy

Find joy in the midst of the storm

Live each day like it is your last

Peace means more than money can buy

Make the impossible things possible

For there is

Nothing impossible with God

Crucified

Hang on a tree

Insert the nails in the hand

The feet as well

Take some thorns from a rose

And some wire

Make a crown

Place it on the head

Now take a sword

Pierce the side of the body

Instead of tears

See blood running

Down

the

Face

No words said

just pain endured

all for

Me

and

You

Lost

Walking around in my mind

Lost

can't find a resting place

No peace

Clouds are forming

can't see clearly

It's a dark haze

Inside my brain

I want to come out

but I'm still

Lost

I can hear people

talking all around me

I'm fighting

Fighting

trying to get out

I'm lost

I start talking to myself

Hoping that will free me

no luck with that

still lost

It's time to pray now

I'm getting scared

God

Help me please

I'm lost in my

Own mind

Daddy's Little Girl

Didn't know my father as a child

the thought of him was nonexistent

I was told I had a dad

but never knew who he was

Imagine being a young girl in the world

No dad to call your own

the struggle's that come with that

link to today's time

Not having a man in your life as a child

was not easy

especially being into sports

All the other kids had their dads there

I didn't

My mom was my mom and dad

all in one

Don't get me wrong

my mom was always there

picking up the slack

the ball called

Me

that was dropped

Everybody always say a boy needs his dad

A girl does too

How would she ever know

How to treat her husband

If she never had a relationship

with a male figure

these are just some things that

Go through my mind when I think about my dad

I met my dad as an adult

too late for discipline

too late to know how to interact with a male

Yet

In time for a relationship

Now we are daughter and father

Finally

Daddy's Little Girl

Dear Mom

Today is the day you left this earth

I feel so empty and sad inside

I'm fighting back the tears

because I miss you so much

I thought I would be ok

since today marks the year you have been gone

but I'm not

I guess it took me until this long to deal with your death

I'm supposed to be

I guess happy

because I told myself

Today I will celebrate your life

not your death

but it's hard you know

I just want you to come back to me

My heart broken

in so many pieces you can't even count

people say you really don't know

how much you miss someone

Until

they are

Gone

yes

I think they are right

Mom I miss you

I miss

your phone calls every morning

In fact sometimes I still pick up the phone to call you

I miss

My favorite meals you used to cook me

I miss

you kissing me softly and telling me

baby, everything is going to be just fine

I know I'm in God's hands now

I have to stand on my own two feet

you have left me with your legacy

that will live on for a lifetime

I will see you again

when I get to

Heaven

Love always,

Your Daughter

In the Midnight Hour

Thank you Jesus for all that you have done for me

I thank you for

Watching over me

Protecting me

from all hurt, harm, and danger

I'm kneeling down on my knees Jesus

because I know this shows my reverence to you

I need you Lord

more now than I ever did

Help me Lord to make it through

when people talk about me

mistreat me

Use me

Help me Lord

to be understanding

and not take revenge

I love you Lord

not because of who I am

but because of who you are

Your unconditional love

overshadows anything I go through in life

I'm crying because sometimes this life is so unbearable

I know that you will replace that with your comfort

Your grace and mercy is sufficient for me

I owe everything

I am

what I become

to you

Lord you are worthy of all the praises

I give you honor and glory

use me as you see fit

I love you Jesus

Inner Self

Inside there's a spoken word

Ready to release and conquer

Inside there is more than love

Hands of heat when I touch

Inside the little girl cries

Thinking about what happened to her pride

Inside is a deeper reach

Stretch your arms and embrace me

Praise Him

Let's give God the praise

He is worthy

sing with a loud voice

God inhabits the praises of his people

let the trumpets sound

and the cymbals ring

dance until your cloths fall off

Shout hallelujah

Clap your hands

Make a joyful noise unto the lord

It's a praise party going' on

Credentials

Let me kick my credentials

It's all about the mental

Education is a must

so I show my potential

College grad

nothing less is excepted

No need to brag

Succeeded in everything that I have attempted

my work shows for itself

the reputation still stands

and respect is what I demand

Mother of two

holding it down for my kids

something my mother always did

God in my life giving me much favor

all praises due to

My Lord and Savior

Alive Again

One day I won't come home

I want to experience what they say is fun

I played my cards too quick

cause I was under the gun

Young

Fresh from the pocket

went from innocence to knowing

Now I can't stop it

took a leap of faith

before I was awake

Now I'm ready to cut all tie's

trying to stay alive

Help the Kids

In the third world kids got guns and no shoes

we sit eating every day and cry the blues

Complaining about the cards we were dealt

While those kids have no help

No way out

No one to care

It makes you wonder

Why they are less fortunate

Why life isn't fair

they did not ask to be in that situation

but they are

We need to lend a helping hand

so they too

Will be able to stand

You Can Do It

You can do it

Even when it seems all hope is gone

You can do it

When people say you're wrong

You can do it

When the enemy attacks

You can do it

God has your back

You can do it

You have the victory

You can do it

Jesus left the Holy Spirit so that you can see

That you can do it

Mind Control

deep depression don't know which way is out

the mind keeps spinning

no focus

no escape this thing has me

in a state of confusion

if you didn't know me you couldn't tell

I'm a person that can hide it well

from everyone

even myself at times

it's scary for various reasons

so use to people pleasing

but it's teasing

cause the mind plays tricks

makes you think you're great in the brain

later to find out you have gone insane

Tell Me

allow me to advance

past my circumstance

take me out and show me a new dance

hold my hand and let me feel the heat

whisper and tell me you are complete

tell me I can take my breath back

cause you will breath for me

tell me our contract will never be voided

the warranty will not run out

tell me you got my back

tell me

please I'm waiting

I want to be emancipated

newly created

in an image you love

tell me I can fly with eagles above

please let me hear the cheer from you palm

let it echo from here to beyond

How It Started

First poem rhyme written on napkins

lunch room beat tappin

breaking with slippery suits

phat laces in the eighties when I was still a baby.

tap into my energy

tap into my grind

get behind

and push the movement on

to the next level...

Box 1

All closed in

walls all around

the entrance way has bars

in a place

where there' s no escape

the things in the past

have caught up

how long will this last

Box 2

Inside the brain

very complex

multiple things need to function

gathered all in one place

house in

a head

Box 3

You say I do

He says I don't

You say I will

He says I won't

which

way

to

turn

you tell me

all I know is

you better be right

because at each turn

a situation can be tight

O How Sweet It Is

you shared your goals and dreams your tears

and fears

your heart and soul

I want to be so close to you

If your heart skips a beat

I want to hear it

It's easer not to breath

than to be without you

in death

my body may be no more

but my soul

will

go on

loving

you

forever

Faceless

someone touched me today

when I turned to see who

the wind took it away

I felt it first on my shoulder

then my back

I arched forward but that too was an act

I keep denying I was going crazy

but just then

there it was again

it touched me around my waist

I was ready to give chase

I then looked up

to my surprise

there was

No face

Would You Stay

Would you stay

if you saw no way out

Would you stay

if there was room for doubt

Would you stay

to make others happy

if you're not happy yourself

Would you stay

for financial reasons

or for the comfort of your surrounding

What would make you stay?

When is it time to let go

Eyes

the eyes are the portal to one's soul

look deep and many truths and lies will be told

don't judge my mishaps

Perhaps

share a moment so I won't step back

and make my vision deeper

when you come to look back

into my eyes cause my surprises have cleared up

no longer wounded

no more tears

 to tear up

Sunset

I see a sunset twist

with light abundant

I want to walk a path

just to get a feel

and not having to wonder

is it real

the sun is the soul of the universe

God's light

that surfaced on earth

it has been igniting a guide

makes you smile

when you ride

it's never too far

when at night it hides

all in all it makes you forget

about sadness

or the problems of this world

as it shines

the true divine

is a spiritual sign

that God is never far behind

Momma Said

Respect my thoughts because I think of them in my best interest

I stay still just so I can hear the drop of water

I think about my mother

as she whispers

is that my daughter

I raised up and said mom is that you

she responds by saying oh my look at you

I develop a puzzled face but she says no baby it's not like that

You're turning out beautiful in the way you act

I kneeled down on your brother the other day and touched his head

he cried wanting out of the box that he dreads

being a wright was alright now so it is all good

I cried out momma

but she stopped me short and said I know you're doing the best you can

raising a family, school, and ministry can take its toll

she said don't forget you have a wonderful soul

God's got you I know cause I spoke to Him

make a choice and continue

 to make the girl in yourself a woman

Heaven or Hell

Three minutes from death as I called the Lord

I started saying a prayer to avoid the hell corridor

saint I am not but I have done some good

complete as I finish this journey I understood

or did I understand

this life apparatus

holding fast

to the things of the past

misbehaving was the thing I liked best

lying, conniving and secrets kept

this was not good in the long run

now I have a debt to pay

as I stand at the gates waiting for someone to say

heaven or hell

my two choices

I start to think over my life

going through every little detail

searching for an answer to this dilemma

trying to find out why I'm here

at the cross roads

I thought my story was already told

I guess not 'cause here I stand

with a puzzled blank stare

here he comes ready to tell

help me please

Is it heaven or hell?

Tears

I found my heart under a pillow

every night I hold on because that's where my hands love to go

I dreamt of being at peace

an occasional awaking from the Lord standing at my feet

He said my daughter believe and I will guide you through turmoil

I will make you rich as my soil

I smiled, laid back down and resumed the position

my heartache is temporary like in remission

it won't be this way for long I keep hearing

but Lord come save me

from my eyes that keep tearing

December 3ʳᵈ

You see my story began as a hope that I would be more than my mother

single parent to her I didn't look like no other

deep dark skin I questioned the facts

face was caramel brown but his was black

I was told I was a love child

I was embraced by my aunt to escape

my home life wasn't what I wanted to face

church became my home then I fell short as I grew

came back as an adult as so many of us do

the mystery still was evident, whose am I

still wondered

until

a man came around gave a hug and a smile

I looked at him deep and noticed I was a splitting image of his child

now I got him to myself cause my mother moved on

December 3

Nineteen seventy

Is when I was born

Remember When

I look back over my shoulder

and there I see

the girl I once was

and the woman I was meant to be

I wonder how it happened

that the girl I see

became the woman I am now

not the woman I was meant to be

I remember her well, the girl I once was

I remember the woman I dreamed I would be

now the dreams are forgotten by the girl in me

for I am not the woman I dreamed I would be

My God it must be You

When the wind blows I can feel You

I can feel You kiss me in the breeze

the flowers smell of Your sweet fragrance

when it rains it washes away all my sins

to see You in all Your glory

the Magnificent One

shining brightly

eyes cannot behold Your beauty

who are You?

the Almighty One

appearing everywhere at the same time

my God

it must be You

as I think back to different situations

your presence has always been there

like the time when I fell off my bike and didn't get hurt

and the time where I couldn't stop crying

You whispered in my ear

stop crying daughter everything will be alright

you see

I was not dreaming

this is real

my God

it must be You

I will magnify Your holy name

I will speak with holy boldness

God give me strength to move forward

give me peace that passes all understanding

I am Your child

You are my Father

my God

it must be You

Because I Love You

This is my bible, my holy word, written by man, inspired by me

this is what I am saying to you

the Bible is the truth, the life, the light and my words

the answers to your questions on:

How you should live your life and the love I have for you

are all found in here my bible

it is me God

I am in the Spirit

I sent my son to you in the flesh and named him Jesus

Jesus who was born of the Virgin Mary

walked among men

He came to preach, teach, heal, deliver and save souls

then he became the perfect sacrifice

dying on the cross, that we will have the right to eternal life

Why did I allow this?

because my child..

I love you

then I raised my son from the dead on the third day to show you I am God

Jesus ascended into heaven to sit on the right hand of me

but He did not leave you comfortless

He left the Holy Spirit to dwell inside of all born again believers

this is a part of me also

You have the trinity

God the Father, God the son, God the Holy Spirit

You have all of Me

why?

Because

 I love you

Mental State

I need a little space

a time for a place

to let my short hair down

and reminisce about eternal bliss

I need that space you need to respect it

I need my time

to compete with the sublime

I need to know my own facts

by getting into my mental

it's my time to compose a deep soul instrumental

consider the facts if I act unorthodox

I will be knocked two steps back

every element put in place

for every race

but each face

and personality should be respected with grace

allow me to be good

wholesome only according to me

bad when I wanna be

who is to judge but the G.O.D.

if I wanna shake my hips

poke out my lips

just a bit

catch an attitude because I can

respect me women, children and man

It's All about Jesus

Some speak of Jesus like he's a noun

in fact I know he's a verb

a man of action

a man of substance, agility, and love

some speak of him like he's a neighbor

but he is in the inside, I have favor

people run from themselves into unknown hells

not thinking about the known heavens, so I feel compelled

to spell

it out

there is no doubt

I'm on the right route

so watch yourself

I'm speaking out

I am talking about Jesus

He is the reason

I embody the full essence of humanity

I live with humility

dignity, meekness, and security

He brings joy in the midst of a storm

sanity when you're confused and torn

healing to those who are ill

his presence he will bring so you can feel

His power that cannot be duplicated

He is the creator

God's only begotten Son

the Almighty One

created before the foundations in the Master's plan

came to earth in the form of man

Lilly of the Valley

the Great I Am

Bright and Morning Star

some of the names given

to Jesus the Christ

don't confuse him with darkness

He is the Light

Challenge

I challenge you to respect me as a woman

I challenge you to find out why I'm here

not to look good, so you can call me baby, or say come here my dear

not to cook your food and wash for you

didn't your momma tell you the old days are through

equal opportunity is a must i work and rush love to be touched

and told you love me and such

I'm that strength in the house who knows what it's all about

ask me anything and i will send you on the right route

find out what makes me go tick tock

the rhythmic movement of a clock

the way i move is like poetry in motion

like a skilled magician with the magic potion

I'm hoping

I'm not too much for the average

cause i get down without hesitation

from this church girl to the board room still holding my reputation

no mistaking

me for another

I stand up for the challenge

Live and Learn

I would stand on any corner and claim my faith

I will shout out to the world I am women

but the question is

who will listen to me

I have not even scratched the surface according to you

but God said I can do all things in Him

so who are you to tell me I am through

I say who are you

what credentials do you bring

to change my thing

it better be the passion for Christ

passion for love

passion for putting your hands up above

passion for strength then we can talk

or I will turn give you two snaps with the fingers and walk

sassy I am

see it

can you hear it

of course you can I am that women who claim's respect

if you don't know now

then you haven't lived yet

A Memory

Today is now and yesterday was full of hope for today

just like tomorrow is not a promise of what today brings

but hope is always in the air, right?

see you can get busy living

or get busy dwelling in the past and die

like I told you that was yesterday in case you forgot

but today is a force to be reckoned with

stress

anger

happiness

sadness

missing a loved one are all part of today's struggle

is it worth it to stand toe to toe with a woman or man

is it worth it to stress your points just so you can say

I want to be respected as a woman!

tomorrow brings that hope that someone will finally get it

they need to get it

they should get it

that this is all about me

me

me

don't get it confused that I am conceited

I am not

I say I am not that way

I am over confident of my future

leaving my past where it belongs

a memory

I Feel It

The power of God cannot be explained

you can feel it

all inside your body tingles

you're not able to conceal it

or contain

cause His power still remains

to the utmost

don't fight the feeling

He gives mercy, grace, deliverance, and healing

to all those who accept his son Jesus

the Christ

sit back and feel it

come experience the world with the Almighty

by your side for eternity

never fear Jesus is here

inside of all born again believers

He reigns supreme

over every human being

let your blessings rain down on me Lord

I'm ready to feel it

Whispers

The house is dark

silence is in the room

all is still

a whisper comes

a voice is faint

you feel something

there is a breeze in the air

you listen closely

another whisper comes

your mind starts to wander

as you try to focus

focus , focus on the whisper

a breeze touches your ear

when you turn to grab it

nothing there

I swear

I don't believe in ghosts

but the intriguing thing about

the whisper

it is not loud and seldom boasts

here it comes again

softly spoken words

so light it's barely heard

I know who it is now

a whisper far and near

Say Amen

I can do all things through Christ that strengthens me

Say amen!

He will never leave you nor forsake you

Say amen!

He will fight your battles

Say amen!

We have the victory

Say amen!

We shall live and not die

Say amen!

The Lord is my Shepherd I shall not want

Say amen!

The Meek shall inherit the earth

Say amen!

The Lord is my light and my salvation whom shall I fear

Say amen!

Jesus loves me

Let the church say…Amen!

What If

What would it be like not to be attached?

What would it be like not to know how to act?

What would it be like if I was so secure?

What would life be if pain I didn't have to endure?

What if the cause didn't have an effect?

What if the truth was false but we don't know yet?

What if the opposite is really the right way?

Just what if... God's plan meant for the night to be day?

Come Back

Come back to me my love

into my arms

I'm still here waiting

I just want to see your smile again

Feel your touch

Tell you I love you so much

Where did we go wrong

was it not enough time spent

Lost focus

No attention

The sun rises I think of you

the moon sets I think of you

day after day

year after year

I just want you near

to make my life complete

I won't take you for granted again

Let's start over as just being friends

I'll do anything to get you back

to the way things used to be

Me loving you and You loving me

we used to laugh together

fight together

cry together

We said we would even die together

Do you remember

I cry myself to sleep at night

cause I want to hold you tight

being without you is like not having air to breathe

and not being able to achieve anything

Baby I miss you

Take me back

Can you feel my Pain

Trapped inside this thing called life

confused by the world but must pay this price

a high one at that, putting my soul on the line

wondering if happiness I will ever find

promises made, promises broken

words didn't even have to be spoken

silence is deadly, mystical, and blurry

without form, invisible and scary

the plot thickens when you throw in the pain

even in expressing it the pain still remains

searching for the answer

where does one begin

how does one find a solution

to put this to an end

or does it have no end

no beginning

does it just keep going in a vicious

cycle

until death does its part

no pain no gain

a wise one once said

what's to gain if you're in pain

what's to win if you see no end

will we ever know

can you feel it

can you feel my pain

I Am Woman

I am a woman first and foremost

hear me roar

being deadly with a pen is my weapon of choice

coming out the blocks stronger than ever to make myself known

speaking out clearly with a loud voice

I can't sit back while the men run the world

it's time for women to step up and take our rightful position

on the side

not behind

pay attention and take notice

I am woman

holding up society with my motherly instinct

able to recite knowledge in an instant

I am intelligent

knock me down, I'm still a comforter

I am caring

take my money and my job

I'm understanding

talk about me, spread lies

I'm still loving

I rise to the occasion

take your best shot

I promise to succeed and be on top

I am woman

don't take my smile for weakness

nor my tears for softness

I demand respect

deserve the world

after all I am the mother of civilization

the mother of all creation

strong, intelligent, caring, loving, understanding

I am woman

Your Soul

Express yourself to me

Open up your mind and let me inside

Tell me your deepest darkest secrets

I want to go into your world

Let me go into uncharted territory

I want to feel your vibe

Your inside

the focal point of your being

I promise not to tell

What indwells

Trust me so I could

Reach

Deep

Down all the way

until I touch

Your soul

from one side to the other side

Are You Ready

Searching inside one's self can be complex to say the least

because some may unleash the beast

the enemy of one's soul

let the truth be told

back in genesis is when sin was introduced

by the enemy who seduced the lover of our being

conniving and even hypnotizing the competence of the mind

now the beast comes in all shapes and sizes

all walks of life

some call him satan , some call him the prince of this world

so don't be confused or used

by misleading tactics

are you ready?

situations come to those who are not ready

you must be prayed up at all times

so that your mind

will not come under attack

because of the lack

of knowledge, no how ,or common sense

this world is much too intense

for you to be slipping or tripping

about things you cannot control

God is the true lover of our soul

are you ready?

are you ready for the realness of life

the villains that entice

the manipulations, fakeness, lies that are created

back stabbing, back sliding

the problems that are hiding

are you ready?

How Much More

If I allowed people to treat me the way they want to treat me

does that mean I am better than them

does that make me less of a person

this cycle has to end, I can't allow this anymore

how much more?

I'm not trying to portray like it's all about me

is it

is it the fact that I'm kind and sweet

don't take my kindness for weakness

let me put it to you like this

pay close attention so you won't miss the point

I'm bringing out, about this situation

I will lay it so there is no complication

way back when I excepted this, so there would not be any static

it would have gotten out of hand and also dramatic

holding things in is not good

so in this I must be understood

drama begets drama, weakness begets weakness

I'm just striving for completeness

in my life

full with strife

complication, intimidation, full of manipulation

but I have started healing now

no time to look back, go back

to the old ways

I refuse to be lost, inside myself

just to satisfy others

the outside appearance says one thing

but inside it's raining

sometimes I seat and cry but it's all in the inside

I wish sometimes I could be a butterfly

so I could fly

away from, problems, situations, and people

this pain sometimes is unbearable, unlivable

the solution to this is not an easy one

I will hold on until this thing fades...

How much more.....

I'm Fading

As time goes on I start wondering how much more I can take

the pain is enhanced with every move that I make

God only gives you what he knows you can take

He never makes a mistake

what is all of this suffering for

how much more

I mean, am I being punished for something in the past

how long is this going to last

I wake up to the same thing everyday

praying and asking God to make a way

give me strength to endure

give me unspeakable joy

give me your grace and your mercy

I'm fading fast!!!!!!

give me your word, the holy scriptures

give me peace so my soul won't grow weary

I'm fading fast!!!!

I am calling on you, cause I need you every hour

every minute, in this dark world

where it feels there is no escape

I am waiting for your light to illuminate

to see your great

power, anointing , take over my body, take control of this pain

help me to maintain

my sanity , stabilization of the mind , my focus

to regain your closeness

I'm fading fast!!!!!!

make no mistake about it, I am a born again believer

a high achiever and i don't take no as an answer

but sometimes you have to submit

to be equipped

for the things in the next level

God help me please

I'm fading...............

Born

How far does sympathy go?

How much suffering has to be endured?

the world is quick to judge, yet does not know the circumstances that surround it

this usually goes on until it breaks someone's self-worth

not knowing they had two strikes against them at birth

let me take you on a little journey

my existence was a mistake, something that never should have happened

two high school kids taking chances, being free

that's how they came up with me

conceived out of wedlock, born before my time

when having a child was not on their mind

playing games with mother nature, in a game of Russian Roulette

did they forget

or did they realize the consequences

Did they know what would come out of temptation?

I guess not because I'm here now

struggling with this thing called life

trying to maintain my sanity, to make my life right

at the beginning I was :

born to lose

born to fail

born not to succeed

now the reality of me is

what you put in, you get out

what you see is what you get

and the world has not seen nothing yet

cause now I'm:

born to win

born to survive

born in victory

and as the story goes the rest is history

now I'm just me, doing my own thing

making my own rules

and

waiting to see what my

 destiny brings...

He Is

Who is this baby we are all talking about?

What is the meaning behind him?

conceived by the Holy Ghost

something unimaginable even unthinkable

this has never been done before

but the more, you think about it

the more, you're able to understand

the mystery behind this man

born of the virgin Mary and his earthly father Joseph

in a town called Bethlehem, the city of David

lying in a manger, no room for the king

people rejected him not knowing the salvation he would bring

there were shepherds out in the field tending to their flock

an angel of the Lord stopped by to tell them of the news

follow the bright star was their important clue

in following the star they found the savior

He was in swaddling clothes and his name is Jesus

gifts they did bring to show he was valued

this was God's only begotten son

they call him Emmanuel

He is.... the chosen one

He is....the Lily of the Valley, the Bright and Morning Star,

King of the Jews, Savior to the world, the rock of my salvation

the Eliminator of all temptation

He is...the beginning and the end, Alpha and Omega

the center of my soul, the one who makes me whole

He is...the Christ in Christmas, the reason for the season

Do you understand

Do you understand how I made it to where I am?

Can you grasp the reality of me?

let me lay my thoughts down on paper

born in a world of sin and no hope

coping with the mentality of being black, a woman, and no chance to

succeed

the world did not think I would survive

they just thought I was another statistic

pushing me to the background to the side

but the cooperate world was not ready for me

not only was I a black woman, but I also was free

free to do the things my ancestors could not do

free to explore the world

free to make a better life for my kids

Do you understand my state of mind that I'm in?

the knowledge that I bring

the steps that I take

just to make

it through the day

some may say, I'm crazy, but I'm a rebel for Christ

beating odds, taking chances, stepping out on faith

hmmm...tell me do you understand

I mean I can go on and on, cause I have been here for years

many nights of no sleep and countless tears

many temptations, problems, situations, conflict, prejudice, stress, strife

and evil in dark places

pride stripped, trials, tribulations, hatred and complications

just to name a few

oh I thought you knew

about the struggles I face, I guess not

was it the way I walked, the sounds I make

that kept you guessing and anticipating the next mistake

I'm better than you think

work harder than your imagination can carry you

I Can Do....all things thorough Christ that strengthens me

but I guess you really don't understand

Do you?

In Spite Of

I have to do the will of my Father

Which He sent me into a world of chaos, corruption, confusion

I feel like I'm in a world all by myself, I'm walking around in darkness

Every time I see the light it immediately disappears

Is this an ordinary life, I mean has anybody ever been thru this before

How can a person keep living like this?

How will I ever survive?

I mean I was born into sin, poverty and depression

I'm filled with illusions and visions of what it is to be happy

If I began to tell you what I feel on a daily basis

you would begin to cry

I have to pump myself up to even get out of bed in the morning

praying to God just to be able to put my feet on the ground

but you can't see this because you're stuck in your own world

not caring about anyone around you

just on what your task is for today

That can't stop me

people can't stop me,

 problems can't stop me

I'm.......on a mission from God

don't be surprised

because

behind this smile there is:

sadness

depression

disappointment

selfishness

persistence

perfection

and loyalty

I'm just passing thru, not staying too long

In the meantime

I will keep striving to make

Heaven

my

Home

On this journey through life, I have had many up's and down's. There were a lot of obstacles to climb. Sometimes I didn't even know if I was coming or going. Through the passage of my life I have had many different feelings, emotions and struggles. Times when I just wanted to give up and say forget about everything and everybody, but I am here to say I have learned to lean on my Savior and He has gotten me through. Many tears were shed writing this book of poetry but God was there to wipe all my tears away. For that, Lord, I say thank you. You have turned the impossible into possible.